THEN WHAT

Gintaras Grajauskas is one of Lithuania's leading poets, and also a multi-talented playwright, essayist, novelist and editor. Born in 1966, he has lived and worked in Klaipėda since childhood. He graduated from the S. Šimkus High School for music, and later from the Lithuanian National Conservatory's Klaipėda branch in the jazz department. From 1990-94 he worked in radio and television, and from 1994 was the editor of the Klaipėda literary journal Gintaros Lašai. He has been head of the literature department of the Klaipėda State Drama Theater since 2008. Grajauskas has published seven books of poetry, two essay collections, one novel and one collection of plays. His work has won numerous awards, including the Z. Gėlė Prize for best poetry debut (1994), and the Poetry Spring prize for best poetry collection (2000). His poems have been translated into many languages, with collections published in Germany, Sweden, Italy, Iceland, Poland and Ukraine. A selection of his poems appeared in the bilingual anthology *Six Lithuanian Poets* (Arc Publications, 2008). The first English translation of his poetry, *Then What: Selected Poems*, translated by Rimis Uzgiris, was published by Bloodaxe in 2018. Grajauskas is also a founding member of blues-rock band Kontrabanda and of jazz-rock band Rockfeleriais (on bass guitar and lead vocals).

Rimas Uzgiris is a poet, translator, editor and critic. He is translation editor and primary translator of *How the Earth Carries Us: New Lithuanian Poets*, and translator of *Caravan Lullabies* by Ilzė Butkutė, *Vagabond Sun: Selected Poems* by Judita Vaičiūnaitė (Pica Pica Press), the Lithuanian section of *New Baltic Poetry* (Parthian Books), and *Then What: Selected Poems* by Gintaras Grajauskas (Bloodaxe Books), all published in 2018. He holds a PhD in philosophy from the University of Wisconsin-Madison and an MFA in creative writing from Rutgers-Newark University, and teaches translation at Vilnius University. He has received a Fulbright Scholar Grant, a National Endowment for the Arts Literature Translation Fellowship, and the Poetry Spring 2016 Award for his translations of Lithuanian poetry into other languages.

Gintaras Grajauskas

THEN WHAT

Selected Poems

Translated from the Lithuanian by
RIMAS UZGIRIS

BLOODAXE BOOKS

Copyright © Gintaras Grajauskas 2018
Translation © Rimas Uzgiris 2018

ISBN: 978 1 78037 213 6

First published 2018 by
Bloodaxe Books Ltd,
Eastburn,
South Park,
Hexham,
Northumberland NE46 1BS.

www.bloodaxebooks.com
For further information about Bloodaxe titles
please visit our website or write to
the above address for a catalogue.

Supported using public funding by
**ARTS COUNCIL
ENGLAND**

Cover design: Neil Astley & Pamela Robertson-Pearce.

Printed in Great Britain by Bell & Bain Limited, Glasgow, Scotland, on
acid-free paper sourced from mills with FSC chain of custody certification.

ACKNOWLEDGEMENTS

The poems in this edition have been selected from the following books: *Tatuiruotė* (Tattoo), Vilnius, Vaga, 1993; *Atsiskyrėlio atostogos* (Hermit's vacation), Vilnius, Rašytojų sąjungos leidykla, 1996; *Katalogas* (Catalogue), Vilnius, Vaga, 1997; *Kaulinė dūdelė* (Bone flute), Vilnius, Vaga, 1999; *Naujausių laikų istorija: vadovėlis pradedantiesiems* (History of the latest times: a primer for beginners), Vilnius, Rašytojų sąjungos leidykla, 2004; and *Eilėraščiai savo kailiu* (Poems in my own skin), Vilnius, Rašytojų sąjungos leidykla, 2008; some of the newer poems were published in *Metai* (2016, Nr. 5-6)

Some of the translations were previously published in *Asymptote*, *Catamaran*, *Lituanus* and *Vilnius Review*.

The translation of this book was supported by Lithuanian Cultural Institute.

CONTENTS

* * *

because I'm not at all the one you're waiting for,
my hands, my gait, my lifestyle are all different, and
if someone spoke to me, I would answer differently too

because I'm completely different from how
I want to be in the dark, not counting the street lights,
women, stairs, until my eyes grow tired

because I'm not at all in the place I should be,
where they're waiting for me, waiting in vain
because I'm not at all the one you're waiting for

as a sign of contrition, every evening, I have to say
good evening, how are you, thank you –
hungry for myself, blind to myself, lonely for myself

Illumination

dotted lines shining in the dark –
thought-tracers. I would like it
to be summer, winter, I would like
an old woman to follow me with her gaze
and also for something to finally change,
at least, the season. What I see with my eyes
closed doesn't have a beginning or an end.
A closed circle, a magic circle where
we won't be safe. O snail, lost
in your home, be careful –
empty speech, a quiet
hum – listen closely,
instructively: no one's waiting for you.
The symmetry of rotting bodies, the law
of canine attraction, the foundation of harmony.
To live in concord with your neighbour's
skull. If you have a loved one,
ask her to die. I'm finishing, but it
doesn't have a beginning or an end, this

Winter, a long-legged dog

winter is a long-legged dog
running slantwise across the street
as the snow slowly falls.
There is so much! So many
wonderful things. The stunning
splendour of women, the gestures,
the pedestrians squinting into
the cold, a burning cigarette.
Soot, settled on the snow,
and the snow still descending
from the sky, quiet and white.
In the slant dog's eye
lies a long-legged snowflake,
leaning silhouettes,
the cawing of crows,
women. There is so much,
my friend, that's it!
There is so much.

Grandfather's birthday

people think up all kinds of fun everyday
today, they have gathered here joyfully
shaking hands, kissing, wishing honour and health to all
as if they were not already acquainted, healthy, honourable

don't raise without reason, don't lower without honour
they say, like a dog whose tail exists just for the lifting
wishing wealth and happiness to others for a lark
as if they were not already wealthy and happy

there's no one more foolish in this land than I
whose hand they shake, wishing me glory and health
they lift me up to the ceiling on a lark
as if they existed just for the lifting

Meaning

meaning is
a melancholy little beast
who didn't fit into Noah's Ark
and napped through the flood,
through Newton and Galileo

meaning is
a sleeping whale
dreaming
it's a sleeping whale

meaning is
an exotic fruit

hanging there, frightened

St Lucy gets hit on the head

I look up
and what do I see
but the soldiery of heaven
shimmering down

don't hit me on the head
I say, just not on the head

I look down
and what do I see
but hooves shod
with paving stones

don't hit me on the head
I say, just not on the head

I look straight ahead
and what do I see
but two old women
washing a shop-window
with a brush

NOTE: The persona of St Lucy, recurring throughout Grajauskas's work, is
loosely based on an eccentric personality from Soviet era Klaipėda. An erudite,
polyglot outsider, this man would sing songs for a glass of beer in Klaipėda
dive bars. He was nicknamed St Lucy after his favourite Italian song. This
lifestyle was his path of resistence, existential more than political. Such char-
acters were common in the literature and life of the late Soviet era (see also
the poetry of Antanas A. Jonynas, the novel *Tūla* by Jurgis Kunčinas, the
recently departed, also erudite, 'Kunigaikštis' (Duke) who walked the streets
of Old Town Vilnius, drunk, singing 'America the Beautiful'). [Tr.]

* * *

on that day, if you remember,
the air quivered with heat.
Butterflies were hanging over the highway
without moving their wings, and the eyes
of women went red from so much dust

I asked, then, for the first time
and received no answer

laughing, with the slightest motion,
she bared her shoulder

a neighbour whistled on the other side of the wall,
water was splashing, and so – I came to know
the end of the world

just sun and wind, my friend, sun and wind

I was left alone with my
silly newspapers. Catastrophes.
The second hostage's fate is unknown,
but they caught the bank robber yesterday.

(just sun and wind and sun
and wind and sun and wind)

I asked, then, if you remember,
for a second time: 'When?'

and got my answer: 'Soon.'

Ballad

harum harum said the dragon, waking up
and pointed peaks were promptly scorched
harum harum said all nine heads at once
and the moon stuck a horn out of a cloud
harum harum said the dragon for a third time
then, wriggling his fatty tail, he danced

webbed toes trampled the firs of peaks
roots ruptured deep underground
nine heads bobbed right to the beat

then a knight rode through the ravine
carrying a shiny tool, maybe a spear
his mighty steed, caparisoned in plaid
trembled to see the dragon's perfect dance

harum harum said the courageous knight
and the moon covered its face with its sleeve
harum harum shouted the courageous knight
banging on his shield
harum harum said the dragon a third time

then the knight, steed, dragon, peaks and moon
all shouted – harum harum –
and began to dance

The maiden and the unicorn

see the dogs pant, sides heaving, tired out,
see the hunters with bright vests, see their shining eyes,
see the swamp, see the unicorn. His bed is in the forest's depths
miles and miles away from here.

the land of fairy tales! realm of icy moons, shadows
of shadows, reflections of the bonfire's blaze,
and the hunters warm themselves by the fire, cooking game,
throwing bones to the dogs, tasting wine, silent.

there's no other way, says one, it's like we agreed:
it's either him or us. We're past the point of no return.
The dogs are tired, the horses almost lame, there is
no other way: at dawn we will use deceit.

they slept till morning, till the sun blushed their cheeks
with dawn's early light, and you could see it all:
see the hunters, see the bloody snow, see the unicorn,
and you, maiden, holding the swooning head on your lap.

St Lucy's secret letter to the Master
of the White Scarf Lodge

to die of happiness is a lure
all those middle-ages are a lure
a trumpeting cow is a lure
all that foaming at the mouth is a lure
the end of years is even more a lure
shit yourself while head over heels is a lure
heraldry and the number four is a lure
embrace you millions is a number

the weather is nice today is a lure
through wind and rain it's all the same is a lure
the quarter-to express is a lure
button your fly because is a lure
completely nuts because that's how it goes is a lure
the sum of achievements in a museum is a lure
derything you evo is lanity is a vure

I like you very much is a lure
the first class handicap legless stump is a lure
the second class handicap legged leg is a lure
to lure your eyes to her legs is a lure
our *underground* father who art in heaven is a lure
when nothing exists at all for all time is a lure
which of us is more foolish is likewise a lure
both of us are more foolish is a number

Soft snow poem

there are barbers and buses,
there are women saying 'I know you',
there are winters, like now

there are streets,
and orange sellers
of oranges

there are quiet madmen, I know one,
it's snowing outside the window, winter,
as I said.

there are houses, and in the houses
there are many
many things

there are screws, and there are nuts.
You can screw them tight, take them
out, entertainment for boney fingers.

there are days every morning
and nights every evening,
for how could it be otherwise.

probably there are also books, at least one,
surely there are readings over the shoulder,
furtive,

a monotonous adventure.
And that's it, there's nothing else?
nothing. Then what, then what.

St Lucy among the Hyperboreans

the land, to tell you the truth, is a desolate waste,
peaks smoothed out, everything one single bottom,
plinths without heroes. Nevertheless, dying here
is also hard, but as long as you have the dexterity
to avoid the Finka knife of an infidel, you'll live,
and what sorts do here still live – legless, handless,
headless... and their gods are different as well, sneaky,
nosy, the strongest being somewhat similar to
the sooty blacksmith Hephaestus, though this one
is much angrier. They celebrate in their own way,
drinking and crying, not really knowing why,
they're sad, they say, so there it is, strange customs,
but what else can you do in a land where
(I'm embarrassed to say) the women are sluts,
and the men petty thieves. Indeed. But dying here
is also hard.

Heat

heat and the hardly felt stench
of rubbish skips, a fallen
button sunk into asphalt, the still,
sticky air scorching your nostrils,

congealing laundry and people. You
must move your hand to believe
you're not a jewelled inclusion in this scene:
a few factories, smokestacks in the heat –

I feel sick, just thinking, sitting
on the curb, can't smoke, nauseous
from the quivering air, the distant
crying of a babe, so I just sit,

unmoving, and a troop of teens
skates by, dressed in rags like
some kind of bedouin tribe, screwing
their eyes at me in challenge,

etching endless circles, edging
closer and closer with flashing glances,
full of the sap of life, its sweat, armoured
with quick curses that, god damn, I deserve

just sitting, stunned, unable to believe it,
slowly growing old

Pipe organs

the little ones whistle like waxwings
and the biggest barely play,
some fifteen feet high, just
moving air around

and the polyphonic pipes –
not bigger than a straw

it's frightening to touch them –
human warmth
can warp them out of tune

there are wooden ones too, rectangular
like bird boxes with plugs, handles, leather

music would sound so thin
through a swallow's bone

you could die
all whistled out

I don't dance

it seems you work so hard to move
those legs and elbows, really trying,
but one just laughed, and the other
openly said – you can't dance

you can't dance, and that's that.
For some time, you still tried,
but it came out all the same,
the caperings of a madman

so you just waved goodbye to all that,
even rejected the prettiest ones
coldly, as if you were made
of different stuff: I don't dance

that made you seem arrogant
for a while, aristocratic even,
and some were impressed: what
bearing, what pride: I don't dance

you reassured yourself that so many
of God's creations don't dance: toads,
cockchafers, turtles, centipedes,
hippos, leviathans, even cats

but the best dancers are those little
white doggies, maybe poodles,
yet even for them, it's a real
pain in the arse: they're placed

on a hot tin sheet, so they dance.
What else can they do? Maybe even you
could learn to dance like that, lifting
your burning feet faster, faster

the little dog's life is a sad one,
and yours isn't much better, yet
when the time comes, you too will dance
for death, dance like you know how.

How to defeat a berserker

First, you have to make him mad,
make fun of him, curse him out,
until froth flows from his mouth

then place a shield in his hands
and see if he begins
to rabidly bite the edge

if so, then give him a sword,
carefully, and quickly banish
all his foes from sight

and the berserker will bite his shield
in fury, repeatedly, for a while,
but then he'll get to thinking

and now you'll be able to sit him down
in the heat of the sun with a crust
of bread, and let him munch and crunch

but don't think for a moment
you know how to defeat a berserker

after all, no one can defeat
such a berserker
not even a berserker

God's frequency is 50 Hz

sitting in the barber shop, foamy-jawed
listening to FM 91.4 MHz

some water gets into the gadget
and 220V blasts through his brain
so that even his saliva begins to fizz

and then he swears by all that is holy
that he heard most clear of clear
the Vatican radio announcer say:

'You've been listening to the voice of God.'

How it all happened

Write everything down exactly as it happened

A POLICEMAN

I was in town, yesterday, for the hell of it,
just to walk a bit, nothing wrong with that

what's there to hide? sometimes I like
to be a little lazy, or to just

wander the streets, for the hell of it,
I don't need to see art, or stores

this way, you can greet someone, even
a complete stranger, it's interesting

so, I was walking, yesterday, and something
caught my eye, I stopped at the corner

and I heard this voice: don't move, don't move
a muscle, we'll fix you up good, just you wait.

In high grass gazing at the sky

what's this now? Maybe I needed
the heat to burn, some nauseating smell
in order to find myself, having forgotten
everything that is necessary, already, then

with the small letters, i don't know
anything else worthwhile, but i need to write
in the lower case, to be less affected,
and look how it's working, with black

fingers, runny nose, forgetting everything.
Now, I just see those fingers. It's terrible
that half the best telling is done. Fingers
are, after all, a part of your best hand.

So mad! I'll die from myself, biting off
a head, who can say, it's a shit-eating
organ. Jesus, roll me the ball,
whistling through the air, it don't matter

to no one, only it hurts after drinking,
oh how I'd croak if someone recognised me,
I was so mad! Unhealthy, whatever you think,
finished even, not recognising myself, well,

not easily: my letters, as it happens, seep through
with difficulty and you can't complain, can't
get mad without falling on the grass, on
rain-soaked cow pies without cows, how now?

but I'd love to yell at the sky, that whore,
stretching myself tall on my shitmeadow,
I'd eat the crust off, with blacked fingers
on the road, how I'd scream, how I'd die

Battleships

We draw a square. Ten by ten.
A water world for a one day fleet.
We forget our rotten test scores.
A fight now roils on a graphed sea –

the paper fleet, marked by crosses,
travels to the deep. I'm afraid. Tell me:
what's left when the boats go down? –
spume and scales and naked bones.

* * *

now, it doesn't matter, the weather outside the window,
rather, the opposite. Gazing like this, one can go blind.
The most sensitive fingers become bone phalanges,
and the coughing bookworm rises into the sky on dust

now, it doesn't matter, so only the game is left,
a card lost under the table, spiteful laughter.
Having lost oneself, there are still the losses of others:
he died, and the queen of hearts marries the king of clubs

now, it doesn't matter that the cards are marked,
that the players have the same coats, masonic signets.
It's an old game: king, queen, jack.
These days are like that. Not the worst days yet.

The comic strip

what a strange comic strip
my life would make

all the little pictures would show
a long journey on a dusty road,
the slow movements of an eye,
bentgrass on the side of the road

all the little pictures would show
the reins between my knees,
and above my head, in a white
balloon, the text: hmm hm hmmm,
ladida do da, and polite
albeit dignified nods
to passers-by on the road

all the little pictures would show
the whip in my boot, drooping eyelids,
the fallen corners of my mouth,
and the horse's massive rear

so you drive and you drive,
driving along, you drive

from one frame
to the next

* * *

to look for insults
so you could get angry
like a mythological lion,
to be more alive than the living
and more dead
than the dead,
to become refuse, a knave, to consider
various possibilities, to learn coldly
and to choose precisely,
to strike quickly and accurately, to bite
better than a snake, almost
not even touching, to rot to death
slowly, feeling schadenfreude
on a pile of shit,
to scorn oneself, not her,
loving so much that you hate me,
wiping away
tears of rage
to say: better to die
and live, and again, and again
one's life anew,
to live, mincing, grimacing,
boasting of non-existent things, then
to look childishly into her eyes and ask –
maybe you know what's happening to me?

It's him

It's him who takes the lemon out of your tea
It's him who gnaws the legs of your table
It's him who turns the lights on and off, walking around
cracking his knuckles

he tosses your children up to the ceiling
calls your friends at four in the morning
then smashes a bottle onto the wall and
pees in the sink

he's an atheist by nature, he's god's bane
he's your inquisitor and sweet revenge
he sleeps with your women, and sleeps
like a babe

he comes and goes as he wishes
he refuses to tell you the time
he laughs at you, laughs
doubling over

he dips your lemon in sugar and chews
he looks into your eyes and says: 'someday I'll kill you'
he looks, nodding your head
and smiling.

Painfully funny now

at first, it happens that
the sky is above your head
more than the earth beneath your feet
later, usually, it's your head that matters
although, before rain, also your feet
and later yet, it gets clearer and
clearer until only the eternal
things are left
cheap clothes
and whatever burns

The ending which probably doesn't exist

To look at your watch and live. To look
better than you should. Because that's all
that's left for us. To look. To be discreet.
To see as if you didn't notice.
The untouched savings are squandered.
Only one season left. For all the years.
Irony doesn't help. That's quite
ironic. Being humane is not funny.
Being good is humane. Naivety –
it would be good to be naive. Or
knowing how to shoot straight. And
some old doll carriage. For practice.
Everything is copacetic. Nothing to be mad about.
No one says: cool it, mate.
No stopping. No acceleration.
Who needs changes, just buy hats of other colours.
Something ended. Nothing begins.
Exercise every morning at nine.
We learn how not to live. The teacher has
a black belt. An absolute corpse.
We fly in aeroplanes. Go for walks.
We meet people like us. We reproduce at pace.
We enquire: who's there? It's me, your love.
What's that? There's nothing there now, my dear.
We are ignored. We are photographed to the bone.
Mirrors refuse to accept our faces.
We page through empty albums because what else is left.
We look ahead as if we hadn't noticed.

* * *

having bounced around the world,
he returned, rich, bringing gifts
in a new car

his extended family sat at the table,
tasting Jack Daniels for the occasion,
politely screwing their faces

the traveller, having downed a few
too many glasses, began, during a lull
in conversation, to complain:

Germans are orderly, the Irish hard-working,
Dutch people are generous, only we, Lithuanians
have nothing to brag about

so his father, grabbing a cane,
whacked him on the mouth,

saying: now you'll have something
to show off to the others

*　*　*

it's already getting dark, but I'm still
on the intercity bus, my head leaning
on the window glass

all along the way, my thick-necked,
rotund neighbour is squeezing and squeezing
me into the corner with his thigh

good God, what an unpleasant chap

further up, there's a snotty teen and
a timorous Vietnamese girl incessantly
chewing some local 'lilac' apples

all the way up front – a pair of older women
from the Word of Love church who tried to marry me
to Jesus while we stood around in Kaunas

I told them that I was betrothed
to Saint Augustine

and now, it's dark, but we're only at Crosshill,
and I'm homesick like a child, I've had it with
acting smart, flinging witticisms

it's dark, and, losing patience, I tear my head
from the window to whisper to my fat neighbour:
'Look how the valley fills with the river's breath.'

Emigrant

Albanian, Macedonian or Bosnian, who
can tell? – someone or other from that Balkan stew

he must have thought, here it will be calm,
but not so fast: after three days he was deathly
homesick for everyone left behind in their
horror and anger – and so he raged

in his despair, growing faint from love
and hatred, sang in a voice that didn't seem
his own, drearily drawling on in his
native tongue (*there* he never sang)

then, he seemed to settle in,
found a job at McDonald's,
learned to speak in this horrid
Jamaicanenglish, but when drunk

he would accost those good-hearted
Swedes with naive blue-eyes: where is
my life? where is my life, I ask you!

While eating a hamburger by the snack bar at kilometer 64 of the Klaipėda-Vilnius highway, I met a learned raven

well, he's beautiful, this raven on
the snow: not one bit inferior
to the one on Pallas Athena – maybe even
exactly the same, dignified without reproach,
a bit of an old-fashioned classic

(he watches with a clever eye,
tilting his Hebraic beak)

you can see at once: a scholar
of the old testament, maybe even
a cabalist – why else those
secret signs under the tree,
those circles of letters on the snow

(he watches with a clever eye, tilting
his Hebraic beak, keeping his peace)

'shalom, rabi,' say I, 'I am
the post-punk poet GG – what
are you doing here in Lithuania – maybe
you want some kosher cheese – or have you
already written the name of God in the snow?'

(the raven quickly glances about,
then says: nevermore, that you,
one more time, nevermore.)

Little Buddha

it's always like this:
out of nowhere
they begin to scream

then, they seem to reconcile

growing quiet, they stare at different
corners for a while, until, out of nowhere
they begin again

so i go and loudly proclaim
that which sits on the tip of my tongue:
tomorrow will be cloudy
with brief periods of clear sky!

(shocked, they exchange glances:
it's a madhouse, one says)

and what more can i do, i,
a class of '66 portable
radio receiver

Sincerely

if you were really sincere,
you wouldn't talk so much about sincerity

you would generally speak less
or remain entirely silent

if you were really sincere,
you'd say: 'I'm insincerely sorry'

or 'insincerely wishing you the best',
'insincerely Yours –
                     Grajauskas'

we would generally speak much less:

laconic

we wouldn't ask: how's it going? how's life?
we'd ask directly: how's the dying coming along?

and we'd answer sincerely: thank you, well.

Poetry readings

just listen – how nicely he reads:
the expressive voice, proper intonation,
he's marked the logical stresses
ahead of time with a red pen –
he's talented, the wanker, emotions
fly like a pianist's fingers

(i like it when one reads as an officer
of the law – these days, only poets and officers of the law
read like that: in a monotone, knowing
they are doomed to spend their time on formulas
that nobody needs)

but just listen to him: it seems as if he,
himself, will break into tears from the beauty

he is himself the bell, the priest,
and the entire church

and in the corner –
a quiet church mouse:
the poem

Poem about the Lithuanian search for identity

Lithuanians are sincere, but extremely reticent

from the impressions of a German tourist

why do they drink vodka straight in the middle of the summer
why do they shout warlike songs, threaten people and hoot
why do they fight, then cry in each other's arms

because it's dismal for us to live like this

why do they eat open-faced sandwiches during their lunch break
why do they have breakfast drinking coffee and glancing at their
    watches
why are they now smoking on scaffolding, spitting down, while
    looking at the sky

because it's dismal for us to live like this

why do they hurry each other along only to be always late
    themselves
why do they meet each other and then separate right away
why are they continuously unsuccessful and only sometimes
    successful

because it's dismal for us to live like this

why do they get up in the middle of the night and stick their
    heads in the refrigerator
why do they get up in the middle of the night and stick their
    heads in a noose
why do they not get up in the morning but spend all day lying
    about in bed

because it's dismal for us to live like this

why do they go to church on Sundays
why do they see their women on Thursdays
why do they suddenly stop and stand like restive livestock

because it's dismal for us to live like this

why do they say: it seems like everything has already happened
why do they shrug their shoulders and say: devil take 'im, we'll
    get by somehow
why do they shake their heads and say: but something's not right,
    definitely not right

because it's dismal for us to live like this
because it's dismal for us to live like this
because it's dismal for us to live like this

so they say, those Lithuanians, and then they grow
silent, very very silent

* * *

i'm building a barricade
around myself

pushing the armoire and bed together,
knocking down the refrigerator

they send a negotiator:
a pizza delivery man

it's pointless to resist, he says

it's pointless to resist, i reply

he exits like a victor,
leaving me crabmeat pizza

the postman comes, saying:
this is a registered letter, sign here

i sign, we both smile –
it's pointless to resist, says the letter

i don't argue, but politely agree:
there isn't the slightest hope

then comes the mormon:
do you know god's plan, he asks

i know, it's pointless to resist, i say,
and the mormon murmurs down the stairs

so i improve the barricade: sealing cracks
with old newsprint and chewing gum

the doorbell rings and rings

the pizza delivery man, postman
and mormon are at the door

what more, i ask

you were right, they say, it's pointless
to resist, and there isn't the slightest hope

which is why we're on the same side
of the barricade

Some kind of Kafka

i live in a former dorm,
a former snack-bar
(first floor, white verandah)
and have a lot of neighbours

four reinforced concrete floors
eat on top of me

four reinforced concrete floors
lie down on top of me

four reinforced concrete floors
re-arrange furniture on top of me

the copse next door is even more
frightening, containing a colony of jackdaws

they eat, sleep, hatch chicks, poop
on everyone, lug intestines to and fro
stolen from the butcher shop – what
pleasures are these, what occasion, what
noise, croaking and hopping about

you see – even here there is a jackdaw
poet: sarcastic beak gaping, all
insincere, the embarrassment
of the entire colony

the mocker, the rebel, tied
by the leg, below a branch,
head downwards – he'd be
a good friend: too bad, he's dead.

What you need to know about life

Don't rock that chair. Listen,
instead, to the story of the cyclops.
The cyclops had one eye.
We have hope, that.

Good.
Now listen to the story of the chick.
The chick had both its little eyes.
We don't have hope, that.

I also know about the black hand
and the white whale. Ah! He's so
white that it's seems as if he isn't
there. But let's just clap, instead,

clap for each other. The whole
circus. Allow ourselves, allow
ourselves to be fooled, you only
need to believe, but not that, no.

Why are you sitting there with
one bone crossed over the other,
take some money instead, here, run,
buy yourself some ice cream at least.

The artist's wife

did you read what that art critic
wrote: 'the practical uselessness
of an artist's creations
is his resistance'

well, no. the artist's resistance
is the practical uselessness
of himself

seriously, no use whatsoever,
cry as you will, he doesn't fit
anywhere, always too big or too small

now, if you want to talk about resistance,
then there's this ugly souvenir here,
come from who knows where: a plastic
eagle on a plastic rock

(and with an inscription to boot: kislovodsk!)

it stands there, stuffed in the corner,
taking up space. it makes me so mad at times
that I want to smash it on the wall
and watch the wings fly off

but I can't bring myself to do it, I feel sorry
for I don't know what, but I do, feel sorry

so I say to myself, when my man dies
I'll put it in the coffin with him:
let them enjoy each other
together at last

Second-hand

Hello, can I trouble you? Just a bit. I've got
some books to sell. Maybe you need some?
They're good. The ol' shrew threw me out, tossed
the books too, so I'm selling – nowhere for them to go.

You don't need 'em? But take a look – just
look, if you don't want 'em, don't buy 'em,
but you can look, no? Lithuanian books too – not
just Russian. Imprints: The Paths of Heroes, Horizons

and look here... Dostoyevsky – in Russian.
Do you know Russian? Aha, you see, and
here's the one who wrote *Mumu*, you know him,
right? OK, for one-fifty, no, take it for one litas.

One litas and its yours. or one-fifty for both,
along with *Four Tank Men and a Dog*,
so you get Mumu and Sharik, nice joke, huh?
But if you don't want it, you don't want it.

And here I thought, glasses, shit, he knows
about books. But if you don't want 'em, someone
else will. Wait, maybe you've got twenty cents?
I'm short a bit for a bottle, yesterday, Slavik and I

pounded a few. You know Slavik, right? The one
with crutches, from apartment fourteen? No?
Well, everyone knows him. OK, pennies too,
I'll take whatever. I'm not proud. Twenty-seven...

Still short. Maybe?... Well, no is no,
take care then. Be well, don't get sick.
Oh, what a minute, I just remembered – maybe
you know someone who needs a mobile? Cheap.

Nokia. It's new, with the latest melodies.
Chistiak s nulia, mucha ne yebalas. Hey,
now what! Where you going? Wait,
let's have a talk, like normal people. Hey!...

Screen

this thing into which we gaze
is called a screen

it only looks flat
but is really like a basket
full of little dots
jumping around like
shining Christmas
fleas

when the dots receive a command
they obediently stand in their places
and muster into 'tree', 'skyscraper',
'Balkan crisis' or 'Leo di Caprio'
(just look how his white shirt
shines – it's because of the dots)

so if you see something
terrifying – don't be afraid,
and don't be fooled

there are no jungles there, no floods
nor zombies with chainsaws

but i'm not saying that nothing is there
(as the benighted proclaim)

there is an endless abundance

of dots

What there is at the internet's core

mystics say a spider squats
at the internet's core

no, say the specialists

he doesn't squat

but really, it's the biggest
garbage dump in the world
full of homeless people
with browsers

what's most fascinating is that
the internet is nowhere

and that's where we have
our addresses

An exercise for summoning happiness

You want to be happy? so be happy

or we'll make you happy

just listen carefully: if you want
to be happy, smile

smile for your wife, smile for your son
smile for the television
smile for the bitter soil
smile for the chair the closet and the mirror
smile for the burnt stew
smile for the trolley bus and the ice cream monger
smile for the psychoanalyst
smile for the meteorological phenomena
smile for your trouser buttons
smile for the medal of St Anthony
and if you can, smile for the moles
gnomes worms and other chthonic
creatures
smile up and down
smile left and right

smile and live,
like a fool

Children's games

they ran around and played themselves
out. I didn't even have to calm them:
they sat down on the floor and started
doing something or other, quietly

but when they're quiet, that's usually
a bad sign – so I went to take a look,
and it's all fine: they're playing
noughts and crosses

'The cross of Christ saves us from
the circular labyrinth of the stoics' –
so said Blessèd Augustine; but back then
we didn't know that, for we were blessed

and now, I'm standing here in thought
looking at children's games. I'll go soon,
but I'll stand a while yet, for I'm curious:
who will win: crosses or noughts?

Not a poem

and now I'll just write what I saw
at the Kristianstad church

there's a kind of tree standing there
with pieces of paper on it where people
have written all kinds of requests and
expressions of gratitude to God the Highest –
some even have drawings, or Christian
clipart, made with a computer's help

one note, way down low, is written
with a child's hand:

'My little sister
died.
      Patrick'

Cinematographic poem

I am William Blake.

JIM JARMUSCH, *Dead Man*

so now I know: angels are like insects,
easier to hear than to see –
wings neatly folded – *water resistant* –
quietly rustling like soft, warm leaves

angels wearing full-length raincoats,
Hollywood style, faces like hired guns

'sorry,' I say, 'is it me you're looking for?'

(one slowly turns to face to me – a thriller, no, a western)

'and who do you think you are?'

'well, so and so, shelter for the soul, bag of th'ol' faeces'

*'ah, yes, yes, I'ver heard of you, heard
that you answer to the call of writer –
yelping and wagging your tail'*

'well, not exactly, when I wag my tail
I'm usually diffident and ashamed'

'But you're a member of PEN, if I'm not mistaken'

'that has nothing to do with me'

'yes, of course, but then who are you really?'

'others say that...'

'that has nothing to do with you'

'I'm trying to be...'

'I'm not asking who you're trying to be. I'm asking – who are you?'

'as of now, I'm nothing, and the farther I go
the more nothing I become'

*'Indeed. So, then, what more would you like,
O Caesar of the Palemonids?'*

'maybe it's silly, but I always
wanted something more'

'yes, that is quite silly'

'I used to secretly watch madmen,
believing that they could tell me...'

*'the password? the code to get you
into the Lord's Directory?'*

'well, I thought I might get closer
to people, you know, I was missing them'

*'a dubious pleasure, unless
you dream of being stoned'*

'yes, I agree with you now, but
I still think it was worth it'

'and what did you do next, if it's not a secret?'

'then, I came forward, like some
first grader, raising his hand in class:
teacher, teacher, I know I know!'

'first grader you say, maybe more like a whore...
excuse me for a minute, I've got to take this'

(and I can also hear it: the mobile in his pocket
is playing *Für Elise* – 'yes,' he says. 'good,'
barely nodding his head, 'it will be done')
'pardon me, but it's time to go, work waits
for no one, it was a pleasure to meet you'

'wait, wait – I, mean, is that all?'

'that's all. the two of us simply had a chat'

'had a chat? and that's that? wasn't there
something you had to give me –
instructions? recommendations?'

'who do you think you are – James Bond?'

'so what do I do now?'

'you still don't get it, grajauskas? –
the same as you've always done'

'oh for pete's sake, and when will it end?'

'when God's plan is done'

Before the crucifixion, they muttered

so, that Christ. Earlier, it's true,
he spoke pretty well, but now
he's gone bad in his dotage.

he doesn't care about us at all. Earlier,
it's true, he turned water into wine.
Now, all stubborn, he won't do it.

he's just not friendly any more, loafing about
alone, in Gethsemane, silent, god knows what
he's thinking. Yesterday, he insulted good Peter.

the collection box is empty. His followers
have deserted in droves. It's interesting, really,
with whom does he plan to build that church?

we believed in him. For who would have thought
that it would ever be like this? Just the other day,
he turned our wine into water, and laughed.

but what a man he was. What a fiery
orator. He could, I'm telling you,
raise the dead.

it's terrible to see. He feels it himself too,
he's not dumb. I think, my friends, our sacred
duty is to give this guy a hand.

When it rains and rains and rains

Well, hello. What are you up to that you can't
pick up for so long? Ah, so that's it – interesting?
Good for you. Me?... I'm OK, doing what I do,
nothing more. And you? Uh-huh. That's good
to hear.

No, I don't know anything about it. What?
For a long time. Well, somehow, he'll pull through.
He always pulls through. Although, it is
horrible news. No doubt, I wouldn't wish it
on my enemies.

Oh, everything is somehow... faded.
The weather too. You just step outside –
it's like a cement sack. A bag of cement.
And over there?... No kidding. I forgot
what it's like.

So what's new here... what can I say, the same old,
same old. Everyday. Always the same record,
as if something were stuck.
Things change, of course. The seasons.
Me too.

How am I changing? Getting old,
what else. No, no, for me you're always...
I'll always remember you naked. It's something
to recall when the rain falls. How beautiful
that was for me.

It's nothing. We'll get by somehow.
I paid it the day before yesterday. I'm not
dying of hunger. Don't worry, I'm not going

anywhere. It's just... I feel, who knows,
weird.

I don't even know. I'm not sick, no.
There's nothing to tire me out either. Ah, though
I do dream all kinds of nonsense, like I'm walking
in the middle of the highway with my eyes
closed, for example.

Like I said, foolishness and nothing more.
Look, my account is running low, we'll be
disconnected soon. But I'll call you again,
as soon as I replenish it, I'll call you,
stay there, I love you, still.

An immortal

everyone shies away – they don't like him
in the pantheon: drowsy, decrepit,
rheumy-eyed, a horrid stench
ranging from his mouth

but early in the mornings,
by the custom of the old gods,
he goes down to the mortals
to claim his due:

smiling among the crowds,
looking around, sniffing the heavy air,
sometimes for the fun of it
he screeches –

among all those half-asleep,
the grey-faced, the starvelings,
he's the only one who
seems at least somewhat divine

he doesn't demand sacrifices anymore,
nor worship, elbowed out of the way,
anonymous, like the
alcoholics

he still remembers his duties
and his name: Dionysus,
god of public transport

Victor

when everyone celebrates victory, I
simply turn away, unable to watch them take pride
in their impermanence, those touchingly funny
victors of a day

draped in colourful togas
with gold signet rings, they raise
their hands to mark each other's foreheads
with victory's double sign

but the one who can actually say
that he has not lived in vain (how many
desperate feats, how many
shameful defeats to his name!)

is the one who isn't here. But, cross my heart,
I'm sure he knows what's happening here.
How could that old fox, failed rebel, not know?
Alone with his silence in exile, far from home,

possessed of a sad, sardonic understanding –
you can't take it away. It's all he has left.
It's what has always separated him
from the crowd,

and now, in this land of victors,
I give him all of my respect,
and all of my admiration.

Icon painter

while yet a wee boy,
he knew: he'll paint icons

he prayed half his life
fasted

painted and burned it up

painted and burned it up

finally, he succeeded

O holiest Madonna, he whispered,
choking up from gratitude and love,
eyes filled with wonder

he took that picture, without
any thought – he left home
for the din of the streets

and he lifted up that one and only
picture of his, and bowed
to all four corners of the world

and was promptly arrested
by the first passing policeman
for the propagation of pornography

Radviliškis blues

he was the most handsome man
in the whole town – and tall,
not stupid, and that smile of smiles;
girls circled him like sharks

I had hair down to my arse,
and we were a couple back then,
until he fled to make money
and that was that

he married some Irish girl, an orphan
with two kids: he sent photos –
they're all standing in their dumb
Dublin with big smiles

and he always calls me 'deary',
always writing letters, but once
he sent an sms: 'forget that shitty
life, everyone's cool here now'

I wrote back: 'you know, I like
it best in my own hole' –
and what a dumb mistake –
home, not hole, for fuck's sake

if not for those two urchins
I'd walk there on my own two feet
and rip the eyes out of the face
of that entire Ireland!

The decline of the West

so many products, so much colour
and glitter! It's like in the old
Samarkand bazaar.

but why is it so quiet, no
haggling, no din. Did
someone die?

a music barely audible,
muffled as if from behind
black curtains.

only the shop-girls – as if
it's nothing – say good day
to everyone, crying, almost.

Berserker II

can you believe it –
I'm the one who, before a fight,
would bite his shield in fury

how many battles! so much rage.
so many blows. the grinding of teeth.
so many swallowed shields.

hohoho, the berserker's teeth are dull!
heyheyhey, the berserker's shields are gone!
hoohoohoo, the berserker's anger is done!

shoot,
now how do I defend myself,
naked, from you

The whole truth about knights

knights, every last one of them,
are awkward things: they know
nothing more than how to wave
their swords

if you knock a knight off his mount,
you'll see how he lies on his back:
a kind of comical, gleaming beetle,
waving his skinny legs in the air

(the angry ones drone on
and curse, turning in circles
like crippled tanks)

yes, that's what they're like,
those knights

so now undress me,
my love, I'm naked and soft
under this rusty armour.

I understand her, seriously

...and then she says – don't be angry,
I don't know what to do with myself

and I say – I won't be angry,
I know what you're talking about:
I also don't know what to do
with myself

I tried to play cards with myself
I tried to speak nicely with myself
I tried to yell at myself
I tried to drink vodka with myself

once, I even tried to hold
my own hand

I also tried to do with myself
what I sometimes do with you,
well, you know.

but imagine, nothing came of it,
cry as you wish.

so I understand you, but you should
also understand: if you leave me,
then how will I be with myself –
without you.

Initiation

now, I'm a man. I recognise good and evil,
understand their passionate struggle, their
secret intimacy. When no one sees, in the dark,
they enjoy each other.

yes, they are tied by forbidden relations.
an inexpressible humility. Glances
and silences – who would I be without them,
without you, woman not mine?

I'm a man. And like all men, no one's.
Though, as is rare among men – I've lost
all of my illusions. I'm a man, knowing
perfectly well that I don't exist.

what do you think about the one who
plays with us like this? about how we never met?
or that we did meet once? or that we will never meet?
about what is said to us? and what we don't hear?

now, I'm a man. Yet, one who loses,
having lost that which I never had.
I'm cruel and loving, gentle and fearless.
Now, I'm alone, no one's: yours.

* * *

damn, again with that red mazda
under the window: sickly sensitive as if
someone had peeled off its skin, it screeches
from a gust of wind, the slightest breath of air
on its exposed, bloody muscles

and I screamed like that, skinned
alive, barely feeling life begin
to snuggle up to me –
I screamed, groaned, complained
under the bitch's coarse tongue

then I fell silent: my battery
probably ran down – I thought,
time to rest, to meditate on
the world's noise, as if that would work:
I screamed on and on, even while silent

(from a gust of wind, from the slightest
breath of air, as I already said)

please, car owner, have pity
on that perhaps worthless thing –
it served you to the best of its abilities
and understanding, with all of its
pathetic mechanical powers

wake up, car owner, stretch out
your saving hand – all you need to do
is wiggle one finger and the screaming
stops, so I pray to you,
press the remote control.

Spring on Mažvydo Avenue

a down and out auntie with
a punter dog on
the lengthiest leash –
because it's nice this way
for her to watch
how her doggie runs

and a granddad:
a dachshund at his feet,
both striding slowly,
not glancing about, dignified –
because it's fun for them
that way, to have someone
walk by one's side

and there's me over there:
the fool without a dog,
just standing and smiling

The inside of the coat is the better side

I used to live just for myself,
stubborn: I fell and
got up, fell and got up

now, I live differently,
like everyone with everyone else: I fall
and get up, fall and get up

not much more to it, really

well, I did think of what to say
just before I die

while dying, I will definitely say:
thank you, it was beautiful

* * *

Good day! Nice
to meet you. How may I
be of use to you? I can tell you about
contemporary global poetry, it's very
interesting, about making paper at home,
about the sonata form, the fugue and counterpoint.
I know something about ancient harmonies – both
natural and pythagorean, I know a few good Jewish
jokes, I know how to tell good whiskey from bad.
I can also tell you about Antonin Artaud and his Theatre
of Cruelty, some funny stories from my life,
some funny stories from the lives of others,
I know a few things about knives, the thickness
of steel and diamond whetstones,
da Palestrina, Thelonious Monk, John Paul II,
I can curse out women, everything is due to them,
I can curse out the weather, everything is due to it, I can
offer my hand, offer my slippers, fetch
the paper, wiggle my ears, I can learn
to write poems – though no,
that I can't do, sorry – I can learn
to play bass guitar, not to eat with my hands,
not to yelp, not to stoop, I can even
learn to approach someone like this:
smiling strangely, saying – good day,
how may I
be useless to you.

Whatever they say, what matters is how it really is

if you're proud,
they say: arrogant

if you're obliging,
they say: bootlicker

if you're good,
they say: fool of fools

if you're polite,
they say: coward

if you're generous,
they say: prodigal

if you're ascetic,
they say: miser

if you feel bad,
they say: you look so good

if you die,
they say: we miss you

if you're holy,
they say: swindler

if you're a swindler,
they say: a man of means

and if you're a poet,
when you're a real poet,
what then? what will they say?

they'll say nothing,
suffocating you with silence.

Blind date

Who am I?
I don't know what to say.

How do I look? Depends. To some,
funny, to others, awful. To yet others –
I don't look at all. They would be closest
to the truth.

What am I like?
Powerless and pitiless.
Like a child. Or like the blind.

Where am I? Halfway, more or less, between
the market and the bridge, in the shade
of an old chestnut – but it doesn't matter, you can always
take me by the hand and lead me somewhere else.

How old am I? Very,
I think, some three hundred.
People rubbed their sides on me, so
my skin is thin as paper.

What do I do? I stand,
waiting until you write me.

Closer, farther

they get naked, press together
one to the other as they know best

(officially, this is called
'intimacy')

then they lie, next to each other,
eyes closed, flushed

and quietly think:
now I'm more lonely than before

Person with half a watermelon

everyone like everyone – all aflutter, bags full,
pushing carts with all kinds of meats,
pastas, oils, beer, booze,
shitpaper rolls, but he, you see,

just walks along, that guy, holding
half a watermelon

why just a watermelon? why half?
he what – doesn't need anything else?
must be a madman or a cult member

why half – well, that's clear enough:
a whole watermelon is way too much
for one man

and why a watermelon – let's relax, maybe
he just hasn't had watermelon in a while, and he likes it,
loves spitting those seeds

but why does he look so lonely
holding his damn half a watermelon

he gazes ahead, as if into emptiness,
and he walks as if not walking, but going out

so why am I terrified –

but I already know why –

when he gets home,
he'll sit and eat his
half a watermelon, sigh
and die.

* * *

you wrote, of course, a mendacious
truth
about reality not fitting
reality

you spoke about people
who are not on the covers
nor under them either

when we said, 'quiet!'
you were quiet
but ironically, somehow

so what do we do with you now
like this

I prescribe a penance –
seven dancing with the stars
and three eurovisions

Shaman

When men went to fight, contend, following each other's footsteps,
I sat by the fire and gazed at the women and children.

I gazed and learned. Now, I can finally say it:
All of my powers come from women and children.

The Great Spirit doesn't visit soldiers – what would it say?
Let them play. Let them fight and distribute their loot.

They look at the forest and see the footsteps of their foes.
I look at the river and see what will be for us all.

All of my powers come from women and children.

* * *

yeah, so you're right – I sang and
played out of tune like a fool, but hey,
it seemed good to me, even beautiful,
somehow right

I never told you, but
it always seemed funny to me,
all your serious, meaningless work,
all that running around

how you assiduously and obediently
piled one straw on top of another, how
persistently you keep making others
similar to you –

no voice, no hearing,
no joy – soldier ants and
worker ants

I was always quietly horrified
by your patched paws
by your pale, empty eyes
by your stubborn stupidity

now, look, autumn has come and
I don't know, to tell you the truth,
what's better – to be like me
or to be like you

I know it's autumn and we're both
trying as we know best
and that it sometimes worked for us

so let's hug, my dim
industrious friend, for autumn
is coming to finish us off.

* * *

i was playing tennis
with the heavenly federer

and things were going well
i even won a few sets
i was playing and thinking: god,
doesn't anyone see
i don't know anything about tennis
no one even gave me a racket
i leap and flail about
waving my hands
just trying to evade
that terrible object
screaming towards my head

On steam engines

when a person is born, the body
contains 75-80% water

passing fifty years, the body
barely has 50% of its water left

a slice of bread, and a very old
person, contain 33% water

further is the end: neither bread
nor person – only crumbs, husks

Everything seems fine, but something's not right

there is this river, named River

on its banks, a town, named Town

in the town, over the river, there is a bridge, named Bridge

beyond the bridge, there is a street, named Street

a person is walking across the bridge
and his name is Frank

Maybe something's not right, but everything's fine

there's not a single Frenchman who doesn't like me
there's not a single German who doesn't like me

and the Portuguese have nothing bad to say about me
and the Japanese have nothing bad to say about me

so you see what a good person I am

that's why I want you to know who I am:
my name is Frank, and I'm walking across the bridge

Some more about Frank

Frank is not any old person
Frank is the only one

Frank is the one
electrician in town

Frank is the one
metalhead in town

Frank is one
of two poets in town

(the second was a Lithuanian
language teacher, now retired)

Frank is the only one who wrote
the poetry book, *A Chain and a Wire*

and it's him, it's him now
walking across the bridge

Five quick looks

Naked in front of the mirror

it fell so well on me
as if sewn to fit
and now look –

all wrinkled up

      ❋ ❋ ❋

his frescoes inhabit seven churches
but he won't travel to heaven
like this carver of wooden spoons

From an acoustic recording

the loudest sounds
come from pots
packed with emptiness

Madman

standing on a platform
loneliness in hand
telling people
about love

Festival of the Sea, day twelve

empty

only gulls,
pecking puke

Procession. Fog

foreigners, aliens, pedestrians
sine curves, sailors, soldiers

tow lines, dotted lines, magicians
women, children, men
arrows and orientations

went, went by with the wind
and were, were one, and went

while the sweeper quietly watched
leaning on his broom

the last float float by

with a thin frame of bones
with an old madman's robe
with the old chiton of charon

* * *

and so i wrote
yet another poem

yet another poem
to populate the world

now, i'm walking down Manto street

Manto street is long, and i might
just happen to meet someone

[_ _ _ _]
(for Stasys Jonauskas)

A stick is a good thing.
One can lean on it,
or knock down some bananas.

A stick has two ends.
From whichever end you look,
you can most clearly see – the end.

If you slowly move your gaze along the stick,
you'll see the end come near.
If quickly – you'll know
what the end is like.

There is a stick, and beyond the stick, everything else:
that which is not a stick.
Everything else is not concerned
with whether the stick exists or not.

What's wrong? You can't
make ends meet?

You're just going to go on gaping here
like someone from the loony-bin?
well, you'll get a stick in your mouth soon enough
and all your dumbness will disappear.

After a reading

he stood up, gave a dignified
cough, and asked –
what was the author trying to say with all that?

well, everything the author was trying to say
was just said

you deaf dumbarse!

Thaw

so many years ago, this is all I recall:
a little boy in a lamb's wool coat,
sun and snow

gazing, head thrown back, at melting
icicles, thinking – amazing, how they shine

everything else I saw
for the rest of my life
was just a sombre reflection
of those icicles